ALL OF US ARE SEARCHING FOR SUCCESS

COMPILED BY BEVINS JAY

STANYAN BOOKS

RANDOM HOUSE

A Stanyan book
Published by Stanyan Books,
8721 Sunset Blvd., Suite C
Hollywood, California 90069,
and by Random House, Inc.
201 East 50th Street
New York, N.Y. 10022
Printed in U.S.A.
Designed by Hy Fujita

Library of Congress Catalog
Card Number: 72-182687

ISBN: 0-394-48061-9

ALL OF US ARE SEARCHING FOR SUCCESS

Hitch your wagon to a star.

— Ralph W. Emerson

I got a thing I've always believed in. The Lord will help the poor but not the poor and lazy—so get in there and wail, daddy!

— Louis Armstrong

There is no royal road to anything. One thing at a time, all things in succession. That which grows fast withers as rapidly; that which grows slowly endures.

— Josiah Holland

Keep your face to the sunshine and you cannot see the shadow.

— Helen Keller

The world belongs to the enthusiast
who keeps cool.

— William McFee

You know why a lot of the great playwrights
aren't writing these days? . . . A lot of them
are just plain lazy . . . Why, my husband
(Garson Kanin) and I would be successful
even if we had no talent at all.
Because we work all the time.

— Ruth Gordon

The most honest self-made man was the
one we heard say, ''I got to the top the hard
way—fighting my own laziness and
ignorance every step of the way.''

— James Thom

If a man write a better book, preach a
better sermon, or make a better mouse-trap,
. . . the world will make a beaten
path to his door.

— Ralph W. Emerson

The world is always ready to receive
talent with open arms.

— Oliver W. Holmes, Sr.

Success is little more than a chemical
compound of man with moment.

— Philip Guedalla

Physical bravery is an animal instinct; moral
bravery is a much higher and truer courage.

— Wendell Phillips

Think like a man of action, and act
like a man of thought.

— Henri Bergson

Idleness is emptiness; the tree in which the
sap is stagnant remains fruitless.

— Hosea Ballou

It is not in mortals to command success,
but we will do more—we will deserve it.

— Joseph Addison

Every artist was once an amateur.

— Ralph W. Emerson

Opportunists take now for an answer.

— Bob Talbert

The world is divided into people who do
things and people who get the credit; try to
belong to the first class—there's far
less competition.

— Dwight Morrow

There's no doubt our son is a Rockefeller.
Whenever he gets into a sandbox,
he starts digging for oil.

— John D. Rockefeller IV

A pat on the back, though only a few vertebrae removed from a kick in the pants is miles ahead in results.

— Bennett Cerf

Many a man with no family tree has succeeded because he branched out for himself.

— Howard Tamplin

Success is full of promise till men get it;
and then it is last year's nest, from
which the bird has flown.

— Henry Ward Beecher

When the new Miss Universe is crowned,
where just a second before you were *it*,
suddenly all the photographers are rushing
to the new girl. You're pushed aside and
it's all over. But I can see how you could get
very spoiled . . . So you can't let yourself
get used to having breakfast in bed.

**— Marisol Malaret
Miss Universe of 1970**

I've been successful now for ten years. I've gotten too big for my britches a few times. I've read things and thought, gee, that must be me. I found myself trying to live up to my image of myself. It's kind of difficult to remain in the public eye and be yourself.

— Steve McQueen

The man who is anybody and who does anything is surely going to be criticized, vilified, and misunderstood. This is a part of the penalty for greatness, and every great man understands it . . . The final proof of greatness lies in being able to endure contumely without resentment.

— Elbert Hubbard

Everyone's been wonderful, but you get self-conscious. You have to be so aware on the street, making sure you say hello to everyone you know and don't miss them, because they'd be offended. You wonder if you can do the same things you always did.

**— Pat Matzdorf
(After setting new high
jump record)**

19

You've got to be a servant to *somebody* or *something*.

— Charles F. Kettering

Little minds are tamed and subdued by misfortune; but great minds rise above it.

— Washington Irving

Greener pastures often have higher fences around them.

— Bennington, Vt. *Banner*

I have learned that success in life is to be measured not so much by the position that one has reached in life as by the obstacles he has overcome while trying to succeed.

— George Washington

I wish to preach, not the doctrine of ignoble ease, but the doctrine of the strenuous life.

— Theodore Roosevelt

I am turning 80. Not a day passes that I don't try to increase my vocabulary, read something worthwhile, listen to good music and keep growing.

— Rabbi Edgar Magnin

I never did anything worth doing by accident, nor did any of my inventions come by accident; they came by work.

— Thomas Edison

It would be madness to face life without thinking that things will work out.

— King Hussein

The first move I make is always a good one.

— Tigran Vartonovich Petrosian
World Chess Champion

I will never appear in a picture with my name under the title until I die.

— Bette Davis

Wealth may be an excellent thing,
for it means power, leisure and liberty.

— James Russell Lowell

Without a rich heart wealth is an ugly beggar.

— Ralph W. Emerson

If you would know the value of money,
go and try to borrow some.

— Benjamin Franklin

If a person gets his attitude toward money straight, it will help straighten out almost every other area of his life.

— Billy Graham

When I win a championship, I have the feeling that the man upstairs is looking after me, and I want to give something back.

— Lee Trevino
(Contributing $4800 to a British orphanage after winning the British Open)

Surplus wealth is a sacred trust which its possessor is bound to administer in his lifetime for the good of the community.

— Andrew Carnegie

Houston, Tranquility Base here.
The Eagle has landed!

— Astronaut Neil Armstrong

The value of a man should be seen in what he gives and not in what he is able to receive.

— Albert Einstein

I didn't want to leave a vast estate to my children—I don't want to deny them the advantages I had, which come from making your own way in the world.

— H. Ross Perot

Everybody likes and respects self-made men. It is a great deal better to be made in that way than not to be made at all.

— Oliver W. Holmes, Sr.

I desire so to conduct the affairs of this Administration so that if at the end, when I come to lay down the reins of power, I have lost every other friend on earth, I shall have at least one friend left, and that friend shall be down inside of me.

— Abraham Lincoln

One may scorn success, but one would miss it. Being talked about is a bad habit one picks up. Anonymity is depressing; so is fame.

— Eugene Ionesco

Lunacy is a very important quality in being a successful director. Most of the top directors are quite a bit batty. That's what makes them great. They can conceive fantasies beyond the normal mind.

— Michael Winner

One of the common factors in success stories is the alarm clock.

— Sheffield, Ala. *Times*

I owe my continued success to the Beatles
and other groups. They are all alike and
sound more or less the same. They are so
loud that anything I play is like a breath
of fresh air.

— **Montovani**

Let them call it mischief; when it is past and
prospered, it will be virtue.

— **Ben Johnson**

All you need in this life is ignorance and
confidence, and then Success is sure.

— **Mark Twain**

We can do anything we want to if we stick to it long enough.

— Helen Keller

Knowledge and timber shouldn't be used till they are seasoned.

— Oliver W. Holmes, Sr.

A short cut to success can turn into a trap door to failure.

— Alexander Drey

Nothing ever comes to pass without a cause.

— Jonathan Edwards

Ideals are like stars; you will not succeed in touching them with your hands. But like the seafaring man on the desert of waters, you choose them as your guides, and following them you will reach your destiny.

— Carl Schurz

Better that we should err in action than wholly refuse to perform. The storm is so much better than the calm, as it declares the presence of a living principle. Stagnation is something worse than death.

— William G. Simms

In order to be a realist you must
believe in miracles.

— David Ben-Gurion

He that riseth late must trot all day, and shall scarce overtake his business by night.

— **Benjamin Franklin**

If you aspire for success, do not squander your time reading about the things others have done. It is better to get on living your own life than to concern yourself with what others have done.

— Aristotle Onassis

The intellectual singer . . . never lets go of technique. I heard Maria Callas sing *Tosca* after her voice was gone, and in 20 minutes you weren't aware of it. If I had a choice, I'd take ten years as Callas rather than 30 years as somebody else.

— Beverly Sills

The difference between failure and success is doing a thing nearly right and doing it exactly right.

— Edward Simmons

There are a few people who think I'm one
of the best soccer players in the world,
but I won't be happy until everyone does.

— Georgie Best

Do I *care* if audiences interrupt the
music? Heavens, no! Let them
applaud in the middle of it.

— Dorothy Kirsten

You're as young as your self-confidence,
and as old as your despair.

— Busby Berkeley

I remember when Humphrey Bogart got
$250,000 for a picture. Somebody asked
him, "What makes you think you're worth
$250,000?" He said, "Because I can get it!"

— Johnny Carson

On becoming a grandmother:
It's fantastic—
it's just like drinking a hot toddy.

— Elizabeth Taylor

The lowest ebb is the turn of the tide.

— Henry W. Longfellow

In this world a man must be either
anvil or hammer.

— Henry W. Longfellow

I have not observed men's honesty
to increase with their riches.

— Thomas Jefferson

The ripest peach is on the highest tree.

— James Whitcomb Riley

You can and you can't,
You shall and you shan't;
You will and you won't;
You'll be damned if you do,
And you'll be damned if you don't.

— Lorenzo Dow

The only limit to our realization of tomorrow
will be our doubts of today. Let us move
forward with strong and active faith.

— Franklin D. Roosevelt

Far better it is to dare mighty things, to win glorious triumphs, even though checkered by failure, than to take rank with those poor spirits who neither enjoy much nor suffer much, because they live in the gray twilight that knows not victory nor defeat.

— Theodore Roosevelt

I'm just lucky—extremely lucky—that financial success came late in life rather than early. A young man might view it the other way around. But if I had been successful when I was young, I might not have done anything, seen anything, gone adventuring.

— Thomas Hart Benton

Draw your salary before spending it.

— George Ade

I have earned a lot of money from animals and I think they should have some of it back.

— David Shepherd (who has raised $180,000 for wildlife funds since he began painting animals in 1960)

When I had no money I used to buy caviar, which I love. The guilt I felt just going up to the counter—that was terrible. Now I've got a sauna bath in the basement and an expensive German shower. . . . I thought, "What am I doing? What's wrong with the shower in the bathroom upstairs?" No, you never lose your guilt complex; never.

— Sean Connery

It is not enough to be industrious; so are the ants—what are you industrious about?

— Henry David Thoreau

Vigor is contagious; and whatever makes us think or feel strongly adds to our power and enlarges our field of action.

— Ralph W. Emerson

Nothing succeeds so well as success.

— Talleyrand

If you would not be forgotten as soon as you are dead, either write things worth reading or do things worth writing.

— Benjamin Franklin

The starving-in-a-garret theory is sheer nonsense. Shakespeare was well fed, owned his tenement houses, collected his rents, kept the plumbing in repair—and wrote *Lear*.

— Arthur Ballet

Not the prize, but that which enters into the winning of it is what constitutes success.

— B. C. Forbes

I have yet to encounter that common myth of weak men, an insurmountable barrier.

— James Allen (*A Kentucky Cardinal*)

The way to climb a mountain is to put one foot in front of the other and start.

— Rod McKuen

When a man succeeds, he does it in spite of everybody, and not with the assistance of everybody.

— Ed Howe

I have 13 dependents. All of them have 140 IQ or better, except me. I'm under 100 and I support them all.

— Chi Chi Rodriguez

With faith in Almighty God . . . you can go
forward toward the pillar of cloud
by day and pillar of fire by night.
If we do that, we can't go wrong.

— Rabbi Edgar Magnin

If A equals success, then the formula is A
equals X plus Y plus Z, with X being work,
Y play, and Z keeping your mouth shut.

— Albert Einstein

Standing on your dignity makes
for poor footing.

— Arnold H. Glasow

My greatest weakness, the fact I was never
trained for any of the things I do, is my
greatest strength. I was always able to
remain myself. But that really shouldn't
be the key to success. I still want to
find out for myself if I can play good
character roles. And that's why,
you see, I'm still not a success.

— Bing Crosby

A man must *get* a thing before
he can *forget* it.

— Oliver W. Holmes, Sr.

All my life I have been on my knees before
the art of music. I adored it. I lived for it.
It has made me the happiest of men,
for my work is the greatest privilege and
the greatest joy in the world.

— Artur Rubinstein

Nothing great was ever achieved
without enthusiasm.

— Ralph W. Emerson

I believe the true road to pre-eminent success in any line is to make yourself master of that line.

— Andrew Carnegie

When I started singing the real Negro music, the Negro himself turned up his nosé at me; they wanted me to sing opera. What do I know about opera? The only thing I know is what I heard down South . . . they just stood on the corner singing it. . . .

— Mahalia Jackson

I'm always surprised about my success.
Every day I'm surprised. And I think the
day I'm not surprised, I'm finished.

— Charles Aznavour

The American Dream obviously can't be true. Success always brings bitterness. Success can only make you realize you could have done so much more. You could have, and you hate yourself for not having done it. If you build your own pyramid, do it right.

— Lee Marvin

We live in this world, that is true. But the point of living is: don't be subdued by it.

— Billy Graham

Victories that are cheap are cheap. Those only are worth having which come as a result of hard fighting.

— Henry Ward Beecher

Damn the torpedoes! Captain Drayton, go ahead!

—Admiral David Farragut

Genius may conceive, but patient labor must consummate.

— Horace Mann

I believe that man will not merely endure; he will prevail.

— William Faulkner

From above we can hear the crowd below
growling and grumbling and taking it easy.

— Robert Dollar

Success is that old ABC—
ability, breaks and courage.

— Charles Luckman

If you wish success in life, make
perseverance your bosom friend,
experience your wise counselor,
caution your elder brother, and
hope your guardian genius.

— Joseph Addison

Time is the coin of life. It is the only coin you have, and only you can determine how it will be spent. Be careful lest you let other people spend it for you.

— Carl Sandburg

Never put off till tomorrow what you can do today.

— Thomas Jefferson

Every event that a man would master must be mounted on the run, and no man ever caught the reins of a thought except as it galloped past him.

— Oliver W. Holmes, Sr.

There are two things to aim at in life;
first, to get what you want; and,
after that, to enjoy it. Only the wisest
of mankind can achieve the second.

— Logan Pearsall Smith